A GIFT FOR:

_____

FROM:

_____

Published in 2016 by Hallmark Gift Books,
a division of Hallmark Cards, Inc.,
Kansas City, MO 64141
Visit us on the Web at Hallmark.com.

Editorial Director: Delia Berrigan
Editor: Kara Goodier
Art Director: Chris Opheim
Designer: Brian Pilachowski
Production Designer: Dan Horton
Contributing Writers: Keely Chace, Renee Daniels,
Jake Gahr, Bill Gray, Keion Jackson, Diana Manning,
and Katherine Stano.

ISBN: 978-1-63059-942-3
BOK2275

Made in China
1116

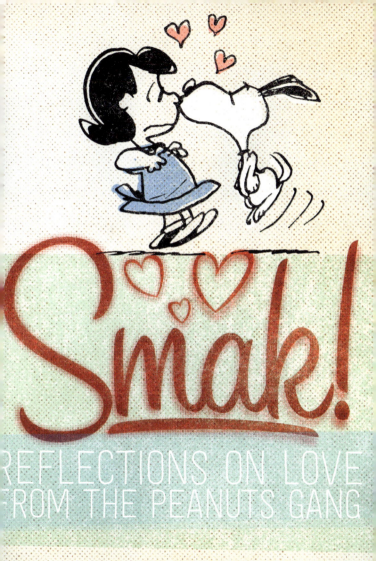

Smak!

REFLECTIONS ON LOVE FROM THE PEANUTS GANG

Hallmark

n Love is...

CRUSHING

SHYNESS

COMMUNICATING

EXCITEMENT

SECURITY

Falling in Love

CRUS

YOU JUST N
WHEN IT'L

THEY CALL IT
A **CRUSH**
BECAUSE YOU
REALLY WANT
TO **HUG**
SOMEBODY.

IT'S NOT REALLY
EASY TO FIND
SOMEONE YOU LIKE,
BUT WHEN YOU DO,
IT'S REALLY EASY
TO LIKE THEM.

THAT FEELING
WORTH
FLUTTERING
ABOUT.

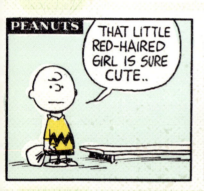

in Love is...

ESS

HOW DO I GET THE LITTLE
RED-HAIRED GIRL TO LIKE ME?

USE WHAT YOU'VE GOT,
CHARLIE BROWN.

BUT ALL I HAVE IS BLAH.
DO GIRLS LIKE BLAH?

I THINK IT DEPENDS ON
WHO THE BLAH BELONGS TO.

JITTERS HAPPEN
EVEN PEOPLE WITH

O EVERYONE . . .
TURALLY CURLY HAIR.

WHY IS IT SO MUCH EASIER
TO LIKE SOMEONE THAN IT IS
TO ACTUALLY TALK TO THEM?

BECAUSE YOUR HEART IS
BRAVER THAN YOUR MOUTH.

MY MOUTH IS A BIG COWARD,
APPARENTLY.

THEN GO WITH YOUR HEART.
FIVE CENTS, PLEASE.

SOMETIMES IT TA
TO END ON "SI

FIRST KISS AND FUN?

g in Love is...

ICATING

THE DEEPER
THE FEELINGS,
THE HARDER
IT IS TO
EXPRESS
THEM.

SOMETIMES A HUG IS TH

A LOT OF TIM

EST THING YOU CAN SAY.
ES, ACTUALLY.

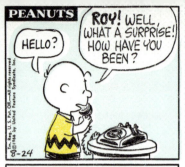

THERE'S NOTHING LIKE HAVING YOUR OWN SPECIAL NICKNAME.

LOVE MEANS
HAVING TO S

OCCASIONALLY

AY "AAUGH!"

A **KISS**
CAN SAY
WHAT WORDS
CAN'T.

SOMETIMES "HELLO" IS THE LITTLE BEGINNING OF A GREAT STORY.

Falling in Love

EXCIT

PEANUTS
by SCHULZ

TANGLED
UP IN **LOVE**
IS THE BEST
KIND OF
TANGLED UP.

IT'S HARD TO
WHEN YOU

THERE'S A CERTA

YOU ONL

WHEN YOU'VE FOUND

N KIND OF SMILE

Y SMILE

UR SPECIAL SOMEONE.

HEAD OVER
HEELS
IS SUCH A
HAPPY
WAY TO BE.

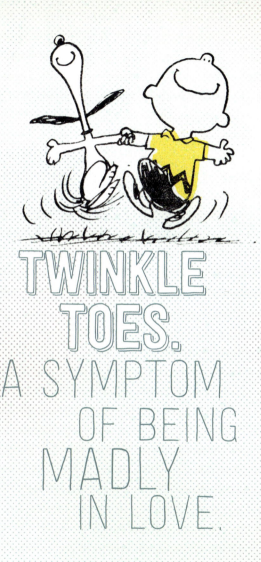

TWINKLE
TOES.
A SYMPTOM
OF BEING
MADLY
IN LOVE.

n *Love is...*

RITY

IT'S NICE TO HAVE
ALWAYS SEE

EVEN WHEN IT'S **MESSY**, IT'S ALWAYS **WORTH IT.**

LOVE IS HAV
WHO UNDER

IF LIFE IS A
SONG,
LOVE IS THE
MUSIC.

WHEN SOMEONE HAS A
THEY'RE ALWAY

PLACE IN YOUR HEART.
S ON YOUR MIND.

TOGETHER
JUST MIGHT
BE MY
FAVORITE
WORD.

If you have enjoyed this book
or it has touched your life in some way,
we would love to hear from you.

Please send your comments to:

Hallmark Book Feedback

P.O. Box 419034

Mail Drop 100

Kansas City, MO 64141

Or e-mail us at:

booknotes@hallmark.com